# Social Distancing

## Together We Can: Pandemic

By Shannon Stocker

21st Century
**Junior** Library

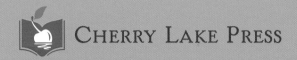

# CHERRY LAKE PRESS

Published in the United States of America by Cherry Lake Publishing Group
Ann Arbor, Michigan
www.cherrylakepublishing.com

Reading Adviser: Marla Conn, MS, Ed., Literacy specialist, Read-Ability, Inc.

Photo Credits: © Kzenon/Shutterstock.com, cover, 1; © Gabor Tokodi/Shutterstock.com, 4; © YES Market Media/Shutterstock.com, 6; © 5D Media/Shutterstock.com, 8; © Pazargic Liviu/Shutterstock.com, 10; © Yevhen Prozhyrko/Shutterstock.com, 12; © DenisProduction.com/Shutterstock.com, 14; © LightField Studios/Shutterstock.com, 16; © Alessandro Dahan/Shutterstock.com, 18; © Romrodphoto/Shutterstock.com, 20

**Cherry Lake Press** is an imprint of Cherry Lake Publishing Group.

Library of Congress Cataloging-in-Publication Data

Names: Stocker, Shannon, author.
Title: Social distancing / Shannon Stocker.
Description: Ann Arbor, Michigan : Cherry Lake Publishing, 2021. | Series: Together we can: pandemic | Includes index. | Audience: Grades 2-3 | Summary: "The COVID-19 pandemic introduced many changes into children's lives. Social Distancing explains this novel but essential concept and gives actionable suggestions to help young readers adapt and cope as we navigate the current outbreak. Includes science content, based on current CDC recommendations, as well as social emotional content to help with personal wellness and development of empathy. All books in the 21st Century Junior Library encourage readers to think critically and creatively, and use their problem-solving skills. Book includes table of contents, sidebars, glossary, index, and author biography"—Provided by publisher.
Identifiers: LCCN 2020039981 (print) | LCCN 2020039982 (ebook) | ISBN 9781534180123 (hardcover) | ISBN 9781534181830 (paperback) | ISBN 9781534181137 (pdf) | ISBN 9781534182844 (ebook)
Subjects: LCSH: COVID-19 (Disease)—Social aspects—Juvenile literature. | COVID-19 (Disease)—Prevention—Juvenile literature. | Social distance—Juvenile literature.
Classification: LCC RA644.C67 S76 2021 (print) | LCC RA644.C67 (ebook) | DDC 362.1962/414—dc23
LC record available at https://lccn.loc.gov/2020039981
LC ebook record available at https://lccn.loc.gov/2020039982

Cherry Lake Publishing Group would like to acknowledge the work of the Partnership for 21st Century Learning, a Network of Battelle for Kids. Please visit http://www.battelleforkids.org/networks/p21 for more information.

Printed in the United States of America
Corporate Graphics

# CONTENTS

**5** **Why Social Distance?**

**13** **How to Social Distance**

**19** **When Will Social Distancing Stop?**

**22** Glossary

**23** Find Out More

**24** Index

**24** About the Author

Social distancing stops a virus in its tracks.

# Why Social Distance?

Have you ever heard of **social distancing**? It means we have to keep physical distance between ourselves and other people. When a **pandemic** sweeps the globe, like the **coronavirus** did in 2020, social distancing is the best thing we can do to help prevent the disease from spreading. But limiting face-to-face contact can be hard, especially for weeks on end.

Car parades are a great way to celebrate and
see friends while social distancing.

Were you sad or angry when you first learned you couldn't visit your grandparents, friends, or even your teacher at school? Many people feel frustrated and lonely during a **quarantine**. It's natural to be upset when we're told we can't see the people we love. It may sound unfair, but the best way to show someone you care during a pandemic is to keep your distance from them.

# Make a Guess!

Do you know how far away you should stand from someone else when social distancing? Turn to page 13 for the answer!

Deliver a letter or drawing to someone to let them know you miss them.

The coronavirus is a tiny intruder that can enter our bodies surprisingly easily. It travels from one person to another by attaching to droplets that leave our bodies. This happens when we sneeze or cough, and even when we speak, sing, or breathe! Since you might not even know you're infected, you can pass the virus on to friends at school or places of worship, or even to strangers on the street. Social distancing helps break that cycle and stop the virus from spreading.

Go on walks or bike rides with friends on opposite sides of the street.

The coronavirus doesn't make everyone feel sick, but some people are at higher risk of serious illness. Those with health conditions like asthma or heart disease must be extra careful. So do people age 65 and older and pregnant women. We need to be extra careful around them. If only one person doesn't social distance, they put everyone else at risk.

Play tic-tac-toe on the sidewalk with chalk. But remember
to give your friend space when it's their turn!

# How to Social Distance

Social distancing means staying at least 6 feet (2 meters) away from others. Sadly, that means no hugs, handshakes, kisses, or high fives with anyone who doesn't live with you. It also means you should not share toys, food, or drinks with other people. To be safe, avoid parks and jungle gyms. Though you can't go into other people's houses, you can wave!

Bring your own food and blanket for social-distance picnics.
Don't forget to stay 6 feet (2 m) apart!

During a quarantine, you should only go out if you absolutely have to. Thankfully, groceries, medications, restaurant food, toys—most anything you need—can be delivered or is available for **curbside pickup**. Some stores require you to go inside, but they'll do the shopping for you before you come. Remember to wear a cloth mask if you must go inside and use hand sanitizer when you leave. Then, wash your hands for 20 seconds as soon as you get home.

# Think!

Name something (or someone) that you think is about 6 feet (2 m) tall.

Technology is always a safe way to connect with family and friends.

Many stores have stickers on the floors at checkout, which help customers stay 6 feet (2 m) apart. Other stores have arrows to show you which direction you should go down aisles. That way, people don't have to walk past one another. By respecting those boundaries, you're being a responsible **citizen**!

# Create!

Make a sign for your door thanking people for social distancing.

Researchers work hard to find vaccines that
help keep people safe and healthy.

# When Will Social Distancing Stop?

Have you ever gotten a **vaccine** for the flu? This shot helps our bodies build **antibodies**, so we don't catch that virus. Unfortunately, **COVID-19** is so new that researchers haven't had time to develop a good vaccine or dependable treatment yet. As long as the number of cases keeps climbing and we have no way for our bodies to fight back, we should continue to practice social distancing.

Some neighborhoods have created scavenger hunts. Have you seen hearts or rainbows in windows? See how many you can find!

Just because we're social distancing doesn't mean we can't see friends. We just have to respect the rules! Touch-free games like charades, Pictionary, and Simon Says are fun and safe. Just be sure to play them outside and stay 6 feet (2 m) away. By practicing social distancing, you're telling the people around you, "I care enough to keep you safe and healthy." Remember, we're all in this together!

# GLOSSARY

**antibodies** (AN-tih-bah-deez) proteins produced by the immune system to stop viruses or bacteria from making you sick

**citizen** (SIT-ih-zuhn) someone who lives in a particular city or town

**coronavirus** (kuh-ROH-nuh-vye-ruhs) a family of viruses that cause a variety of illnesses in people and other mammals

**COVID-19** (KOH-vid nine-TEEN) the name of the disease caused by the coronavirus

**curbside pickup** (KURB-side PIK-uhp) a service offering customers the ability to pick up their order without getting out of the car

**pandemic** (pan-DEM-ik) an outbreak of a disease that affects a large part of the population

**quarantine** (KWOR-uhn-teen) the state of being isolated from others

**social distancing** (SOH-shuhl DIS-tuhns-ing) the act of staying at least 6 feet (2 m) away from others

**vaccine** (vak-SEEN) a shot that helps your body produce antibodies to fight a specific disease

# FIND OUT MORE

## WEBSITES

**CDC—Social Distancing**
https://www.cdc.gov/coronavirus/2019-ncov/prevent-getting-sick/
social-distancing.html

**The Children's Trust—Explaining Social Distancing to Kids**
https://www.thechildrenstrust.org/content/explaining-social-
distancing-kids

**KidsHealth—Coronavirus (COVID-19): Social Distancing
with Children**
https://kidshealth.org/en/parents/coronavirus-social-distancing.html

**Motherly—10 Phrases Parents Can Use to Help Kids
Understand Social Distancing**
https://www.mother.ly/child/help-kids-understand-social-distancing

**YouTube—What Is Social Distancing? Cincinnati Children's**
https://www.youtube.com/watch?v=KXUT62G-IcU

# INDEX

**A**
antibodies, 19

**C**
car parades, 6
celebrations, 6
coronavirus, 5, 9, 11, 19
COVID-19, 19
curbside pickups, 15

**D**
deliveries, 15
disease prevention, 5

**F**
face-to-face contact.
    See social distancing
friends, 6, 21
frustration, 7

**G**
games, touch-free, 21

**H**
hand sanitizer, 15
hand washing, 15
handshakes, 13
high fives, 13
hugs, 13

**K**
kisses, 13

**L**
loneliness, 7

**M**
masks, 15

**O**
outdoors, 21

**P**
pandemics, 5
people at risk, 11
picnics, 14

**Q**
quarantine, 7, 15

**R**
researchers, 18, 19
risk, people at, 11

**S**
scavenger hunts, 20
social distancing, 4
    how to do it, 13–17
    what it is, 13
    when it will stop, 19–21
    why do it, 5–11
stores, 17

**T**
technology, 16
touch-free games, 21

**V**
vaccines, 18, 19

**W**
waving, 13

## ABOUT THE AUTHOR

Shannon Stocker writes picture books, books for young readers, and *Chicken Soup* stories. She and her family love going on social-distance walks and bike rides with friends and family members, whom they miss very much. Shannon lives in Louisville, Kentucky, with Greg, Cassidy, Tye, and far too many critters.